Twentieth Reunion

And Other Poems

By Gladys Merrifield

Dragon's Teeth Press
El Dorado National Forest
Georgetown, California 95634

ISBN: 0-934218-31-5

TWENTIETH REUNION & other Poems

Published by Dragon's Teeth Press, El Dorado National Forest, Georgetown, California 95634. Manufactured in the United States of America.

LIMITED FIRST EDITION

LIBRARY OF CONGRESS Catalogue Card Number 84-70671

COVER: By Jo Bonney

LIVING POETS SERIES, Number 31
Available at $5.00 per copy
from:

DRAGON'S TEETH PRESS
EL DORADO NATIONAL FOREST
GEORGETOWN, CALIFORNIA 95634

ISBN: 0-934218-31-5

For my daughter Gail Merrifield Papp
and my son-in-law Joseph Papp

CONTENTS

III. TIME IS A TUNNEL

***

PROLOGUE:

TWENTIETH REUNION

TWENTIETH REUNION

There she stands in the firelight, my only love.
Her phantom's the one I know, and this its double.
Time is a tunnel toward whose end we move:
Light, distant light. Behind us the gate of trouble
sucks on its hinges, closes dark once more.

She does not see me, stricken, hesitating,
swept by resurgent blood from out our past.
Limned by this moment I'm a man still waiting
in those same torments that engulfed us last:
Not coming back but never having left.

She hasn't changed -- at least not more than I.
The same quick eyes, wide mouth, chin faintly cleft,
the quiet intensity.
                                        We're going to die
sooner than when we started out together
in paths, books, halls, as undergraduates
in a lost climate, in a finished world and weather.

Wine? Yes, it's welcome -- any opiates
while careful disciplines of the years recover
this thrust of reality across a pool
where I in long reflection, bending over,

saw her beside me mirrored, but liquid, cool --
start from my meditation. The moment's thrown
dark as a pebble, noiseless. Its spreading rings
erase the undulant image. Circles from stone
transpose to finite all imaginings.

How shall I speak to her? Perhaps she's lost
the thing I've cherished, our permanent recognition.
Faith is a purchase at the reason's cost
held beyond hazard of place or Time's attrition --
abject and quiet and centrifugal.

The room is crowded, voices fall and rise.
Our shadows in dark projection on the wall
move in distortion like analogies
of inner selves, awaiting extradition
back to the native state, our scene of error.

The trouble, recall, was family, opposed tradition
whipped into violence. We felt the terror
and believed it wisdom that was cowardice.

Rain of our years yields harvests not our own
in distant districts. There's no word of us
in letters or registers. I lived alone
in a far country; in another, thrived,
have half-grown children whom I love and cherish,
wife, home, friends. I haven't been deprived
except at that core of self where visions perish.

But why define? All error's a category
to which we bring our tithes; we give it
hostages; we kneel forever.
My love, our story
is real enough although we didn't live it
except in long subjunctives, in divination,
in marginal mental notes on a borrowed chapter.
How shall I speak to you, an apparition
disturbed by fact into flesh, bone, laughter,
breaking the intimacy of our separation,
the slow routine of devotion to one dead?

You do not see me yet. This new equation
finds me uncertain, excited, full of dread.
Our meeting will be in moments if I go
beyond this doorway toward you. How shall I bear
extremes of the possibility: Evasive show,
schooled in the patterns of a polite despair;
or, struck by so hard a blow, disclaim all pride,
fear, ignorance, and pain -- in a whole admission.

I have no middle ground, once by your side.
We're not "old friends", can make no disposition
of terrible burdens in a public place.
Death is so casual, derelict almost
like my hard breathing and your upturned face
searching the shield "Lux Fiat"; and our host
hovering, a spirit cowled, like centuries...

Reunion's not for us; to meet is tryst.
No greeting or appraisal. Mysteries
dim the vast landscape of the life we missed
and bid us defer, to wait a little longer
for confrontation of a different kind
when flesh is less, is motes, and spirit stronger
and Earth and Alma Mater out of mind.

The room is crowded; voices rise in swarm,
break, dim.
                                        Goodbye again, my love. I might
have touched your wrist, have felt your pulse still warm.

I have uncertain business with the night.

I

CATASTROPHE THAT WAS MY ROSE...

STORY

Deliberate, years indicate
in decades where they go;
chapters spend us that a word
the burden of them might show.

Slow through patient paragraphs
our growing flower stirred
till bursting into bud it seemed
an accident occured.

Catastrophe that was my rose
whole volumes since defined;
in heat the heart exhausts itself
on pages of the mind.

UNDER A ROOF

I

She put her slender hand upon the knob
and paused a moment, listening toward the room
beyond the door. Then as to somehow rob
joy from the furniture, dispel the gloom
within her, momentarily, she let her glance
scan the familiar bulbs within their sockets,
the bureau where she'd powdered for a dance,
the open clothespress door and creton pockets
tacked there and lumped with shoes: familiar sights
that somehow called up courage to her breast.
Thus with imagined strength which half requites
the summoner, she went to meet the guests;
to sit and talk in a platitudinous vein
of politics...Ralph's new wife...probable rain.

II

Sitting there talking in a too warm place
she scarcely knew what words her two lips said,
yet always, somehow, her "ethereal" face
sufficed to hide old glances doubly dead
within her eyes; this passed the unskillful view
of people ... people. Yet it was not there.
While the small company discussed the new
neighbors, or matinees, or the county fair
she said an occasional word or made assent
on something -- fingering her long white shawl
nervously, dreamily, and when they finally went
she said a proper "Good night to you all."
Safe in her room the little sights came leaping
up to her eyes -- steeled for nocturnal weeping.

III

She folded back the crinkly ruffled spread
and shook the pillows, while, without restraint
strange ready tears plopped down upon the bed;
she sat on the side of it, and stifling a faint
audible sob, unbuttoned a satin pump
letting it fall loudly, then its mate.
Her eyes through glistening tears blurred in the jump
of bright gas-heater flames, in the sure swift rate
of their yellow flicker. She slipped from her thin
white clothes
swiftly, seeking refuge in the shawl
of night, and walking lightly on her toes
pressed the black button on the bedroom wall;
the small gas-heater in her usual route
she turned, then heard it pop and sputter out.

IV

The world was changed then as the long green shade
she lifted. Night air poured about her face
and moonlight with its frayed spangles played
upon her eyes. And to its same old place
a light came, sitting there beneath her brows
like a right queen deposing an imposter;
and night -- a fairy godmother who allows
her child great bliss, only to call her foster
with dawn -- cast an old spell. Swiftly it came
and she by the open window, in her thin gown,
forgot the intervening days of pain,
the stinging bitter gossip of the town,
forgot she was divorced, her nineteen years,
which seemed like hundreds; and her futile tears.

V

Suddenly it was many months before
without this shingled roof above her head,
without the world beyond the bedroom door
to stifle her thoughts of things he sometimes said:
"Please buy a red dress with a full skirt
or a white fluffy one with a purple sash!"
Red! With her hair! Purple! It would almost hurt,
yet those indiscriminate words like a white ash
of something naively precious, lay in her palm
a moment. With the same old wordless craving
which burned so from the first, from which no calm
could come from any possible source, saving
himself who made her crave, she calmed her want
recalling words. (But O, they were a taunt!)

VI

Yes, he was gone, and from advised commands
which bade her strong blood quickly rise and leave
him as an episode, she had loosed her hands
from his. Yet as she made herself believe
on the parting day that what folk hourly said
would change in her heart, *would change,* she even then
knew that her marriage was but lawfully dead.
Then...as she left him, knowing not when again
their eyes should meet, something in his swift gaze,
amazing, weaving intricately, shone
in silver threads, sealing her countless ways
in mail invulnerable, which he alone
could shatter. Thus she lived so strangely gird
in steel invulnerable, save to his word.

VII

"Too much", she thought, "too much of bitter pain
and many years in months to pay the price
of love impetuous" -- and she must feign
by day to have no thought save of advice.
Oh, how she longed to comfort him again
as she had done for woes of his before --
Now, there was so much more than had been then
to soothe, or hear contrite confessions for.
She almost felt his head upon her breast,
his breath on her neck, half touched his rumpled hair
which smelled of pungent barber's oils; but lest
such reminiscence put her in despair
more poignant for memory of its sweet
reality, she counted arc-lamps down a street.

VIII

The breeze grew cool and shivered through her light
garment which caught the air. The night came down
suddenly dark with dew, and the lamps, despite
their yellow glow, grew dim out past the town.
She turned toward the walnut bed with its gleaming sheen
of white sheets radiant, where her body slid
through their long coolness. Then she thought, "Nineteen
is young to be dead . . . I wonder what he did
today . . . A purple sash! . . . I am so
weary . . . It is night . . . night . . . There was a kiss
once . . . a kiss! Please let me touch you once. O!
why is life . . . like . . . this?"

With morning she made her bed and dressed once more
then turned the glass knob of the bedroom door.

ULYSSES

Only Ulysses heard the sirens sing.
Who knows but that the maidens' song remained
magically suppliant, yea, as maddening
as when he writhed upon the masthead, chained?
Who knows but that the warrior, in remote
declining summers, raised his voice above
the laughter of his wife, to catch a note
untouched in all the music of their love?

Somehow I hear Ulysses in his lonely
twilight vigil, as he strives to hum
a snatch of tune to which he listened only:
a poignant echo, not of Ilium.

And as he sings these bits of melody
the laughter dies upon Penelope...

DIMENSION

Forever golden
standing in the sun
all time hushed round you,
the earth stopped still,
no season turning –

O love, how bright,
how clockless, undiminished
you and your world. Crystal air
like cool fire surrounds you.

OBDURATE

I cannot chisel you a grave
hard enough
nor cold enough
though of stone.
No tomb is chill or obdurate
compared to you;
no angle is angular
against your own.

EFFIGY

Perfectly she lies alone
in rigid, inexpressive stone
upon a soul's domain.

Her sightless eyes are wide to greet
those passing seasons which repeat
their ancient drought and rain.

Like flesh that guards the sacred mind
she lies as vulnerable and blind
as inarticulate

to utter forth the blasphemies,
the passions, prayers, and ecstasies
of some inviolate

and sealed-up thing below her head.
She pillows here upon her dead,
her dust-delivered own.

Like her, my chiselled flesh belies
the agony and rage that cries
a madness through the bone.

REJECTION

I would wed you were it not for the moon
which is more fair
or for the silver lines of rain
which I cannot share.

I would kiss you were it not for pollen
more potent, drifting past my lips
or for the melancholy fragrances of petals
which slightly eclipse

your perfumed words.
O lover,
return when the moon goes;
call not above the wind
while one leaf shows.

MILL POND

Find me by the mill pond
where I lay when I was young.
Elms and I leaned over, saw
ourselves transposed, made snug among
clouds drawn down from far above us
to merge the water with the sky.

It is good, good to live, said I
who lay with every element
above, below, reflected: house and fence
and sudden birdflight and my aqueous face
close to the blowing clouds, the fish below,
made timeless all in a warm and daily place:
defined, defended
by circumference.

Find me by the mill pond,
the moving sky pressed over,
the world waiting just beyond
for me, its new rover
who now with wounded side
and broken hand
tend first a time that died:
my earliest lover.

REPERTORY

I lie at midnight on the grass
and watch the sky's event;
on lightyears' stage the stellar ones
enact their Firmament.

Such avid pulse this heaven projects
it pounds within my wrist
as if Aldebaran's fingers probed
the wonder I exist . . .
or that I reached, past nebulae,
the nothingness I missed.

II

SEASONS OF CHANGE...

SEARCH

Gone, gone.
Nettle and red woodbine
rove pocked headstones;
but you did not die.

The road winds on.

Not under elms
cracked gold, whispering;
nor in the house
where high summer rooms
pale over, recede,
gray toward the cold season.

Not in meadows
brittling, nor by slant stalks
casting long shadows,
nor on the round hill,
nor in any distance
seen from its summit.

Not on any horizon,
dusk blazing up
mirror cold
scattering cold flame
on cirrus clouds:
curdling the sundown sky.

RAIN

Waking, I heard rain
speak with continuous fervor
across the night.
A broken rhythm was her sudden sigh
caught and disowned;
the measured voice moved on
in long conjecture, counsel, anxiety.

Sleepless, since heaven had grown articulate,
I listened to her urgent syllables
across the dark meadow, down the road;
I leaned against my window like a lover;
I watched the garden, drenched with her murmuring
and the grass disturbed beneath her restless voice.

My hand reached out and felt
secret night in the boughs of my tree;
my hand lay on the wet bark,
my hand was wet with rain,
dark with night's dappling:
I touched my brow with it
in cool baptism.

Count me dead when I no longer care
to put my hands on the rain
or mark my forehead with rain from the tree's bark;
when I no longer put my mind
to the rain's ritual
nor wrest a probable word
from all that shining language.

TRANCE

Iris, columbine, Queen Anne's lace,
clover and lilac flower --
I see them now
from winter's distance as I see your face,
as I see leaves on the black maple bough
and bees in swarm
across this desolate place.

Syllables of water from the stream
and the close voice of evening
soft and warm
I hear in winter's silence,
in winter's storm,
like your still voice going on
and on in dream.

Seasons are cleaved, various yet uniform
where strikes them through
this fixed persistent beam
arrested forever:
the gasp, the wild alarm.

A WILD PLACE AT MIDNIGHT

Ambiguous warning:
the doe's heart beats faster.
A leaf spins down, caught on a web.
Trapped, noiseless, it turns in the air,
taunting the famished spider.

The hare stops, freezes, alive only
in the small pulse of her throat.
Was it the outmost fragment of an odor
distilled through bracken and grass,
sieved by brittle twigs,
dispersed by the wind –
to terrorize awhile in vanishing?

The poised waterfowl at the pond's edge
plucking one outspread wing
grows rigid, hewn of stone,
her round glassy eyes fixed,
wing taut.
Did a ripple alter faintly the solitude
of the marsh beyond as a cattail fell,
as a tall weed bent over?

Unwilling Nature
mimicks the absent hunter,
propounds crisis,
impels rehearsal,
evokes remembrance.

AUTUMN LIGHT

Dusk comes earlier, earth revolves
slower -- waits in brittle leaves
a shuffling breeze, a lingering bird
to quit the quiet eaves.

Light strikes low this longer beam
from sundown to the grass
that in an amber amnesty
our rooted selves might pass;

might pass through columns built of motes
the urgent evening cast
to dissipate chronology
and magnetize the past;

might feel a tidal tolerance
lift time from off our eyes
and let us have awhile our dead,
and talk, without surprise;

without surprise, continuing
as we were last disposed,
the sentence interrupted,
the pending matter closed;

while slow a maple leaf spins down
of all its kind alone
and quick a whirring wing fans out
from its uncertain home.

LETTER FROM OCTOBER

In such a missive rain of leaves
as scudded through the air
and brittle lay about my feet
or blew across my hair
like flocks of birds in dire unrest --
there settled one apart;
it clung upon my breast like some
lost message to my heart.
Wherefrom its beauty, browned and curled,
as beating, too, it lay –
I read you somewhere in the world
with only this to say.

MAN IN A STORM

At sundown on the wooden wintry porch,
his cold hands pocketed, he stands to wait
(withdrawn from critical destinies indoors).

Sun-flames lick the icy sky, abate,
surrendering distance to the storm's erosion
while "Wait!" cries his heart. The answer gathers.

Hear how nervous and upward in the thickening sky
currents in sworl give promise. Rushing near
on air's loosed wings the Word, his need, is borne,
wrenched from its mooring in his own deaf past:

now in these barren tree-shapes, genuflecting,
now on this wind his urgency makes fast
(always alone and secretly expecting)
crescendo roars.
                    Nature turned roving Why
gives frenzied promise. He its listener
hears hope onrush, grow deafening, now pass by.

AFTER HARVEST

Seared grass
lies on the yellow dust.
Hollow stalks are vibrant
and dead.
Parched shadows kneel in supplication
to the thundering gods of rain
and of winter.

Like autumn's season my short life span
ends
at the time of harvest.
My soul has sipped
the sweet nectar of its season
but now I kneel with nature
for the gourd is dry . . .

Like the supplicating shadows
my soul, thirsting,
leaps at the stroke of the Harvester
toward the eyes of Cressida . . .
toward the dust of Helen . . .

CHURCH SUPPER: NEW ENGLAND

Shiny-white the tablecloths
beneath these feasting plates;
cold the hall, guests not yet come;
dim the banquet waits.

Altar, Bible, throne-like chair,
careworn, pushed aside,
make way for such festivity
as heavy hearts can bide

wrapped up in cold and hard-worked hills
with yet a sparse content.
Now gather men disposed to life
wherever it waits or went.

NOCTURNE: FULL MOON

Lunar cyclops! O an astonished eye
dilates in fleeting fullness, stares again
on pitted topsoil of the scuffed century.

Powdery compost blackening out of men
this lightyear changes with foreshortened term
to denser diamond ore, that was a face:
pain its brief fossil, its aerating worm.

Whatever antidote there is to death
is here, all here in brutal quickness:
feast, family, crowd, war.

Gamut of speculation adheres to the immovable proud
geology of mind: strata of conversation,
Troy on Troy, building but never ended.

Cherish Time. This is the Time that roved
also the Ptolmies' starfields, wended
our way in hasteless need, moved
like slow sheep grazing and forever grazing.

O cool poc-healed eye! The cratered fullness
searches out fissure Time, a lightwell, gazing
in each successive window's century:
surprising with light the scholar interrupted
in courteous discourse with his Nemesis.

Down . . . down through Rome, Byzantium, and Greece,
through Egypt down and into Genesis
the beam's long shaft descends, neutral and roving.

Limned is the deepmost cellar's habitant, speaking almost;
speaking through rotted sandals.

WINTER THOUGHTS

Evening mist comes up from the marshes,
up from the meadows; light grows thin.
Night will find the bare elms' branches.
I must light my lamp within.

The road grows dim with a slow sun's failing,
wild and distant the meadows lie;
tilled by my hand, the fields grow foreign
stricken with terror's alien sky.

My heart stands still and my heart's a stranger
dark and sudden in a quiet breast;
home is my wilderness, home is my danger:
I, the unbidden guest.

LATE SNOW

I prayed for winter, for a winter of heavy snow;
I waited long for my season.
Autumn delayed it endlessly this year: October stayed
Like a fire that would not go out
tormenting me almost beyond reason.

I counted the falling leaves sometimes, to employ
my mind;
Ophelia walked among them. The fire still burned
against water and sand
and my breath blown on it; my breath inspired
its burning.
I turned away, I would not look, but still it burned,
burned and consumed me.

Today the snow has come, it has fallen all day,
covering the wound of the fire, the waste,
the blackened branches.
Now at evening under a sky like smoke the earth
lies drugged and comforted. At last
the mission of mercy has arrived, set up
its tent upon the ravaged field, attended
infection with its sterile passionless skill.

I watch at my window; I watch the soft snow fall
profuse as rain, unsparing, profligate;

it has come late this year but unlimited, whirling,
crystalline, each crystal starred and stamped
separate, the die cast in heaven.

Earth is concealed at last, inviolate, covered;
she is winter's patient, who blankets her illness,
dresses the knitting scar, permits
once more the wrecked channels of her blood to flow.

Quiet she lies beneath the cool gloved hand, undone
of fever;
the snow is undiminishing, deep-burying, hurried,
prodigal.
This is the restoration; a white sleep blankets her.
There is no more to think of till the thaw comes
and the trees quicken on every hillside,
their green branches outstretched like lovers' arms.

HOME

Home is remembered,
home is yet ahead;
find if you can
its dappled door tonight;
lift its latch
and breathe familiar air;
stand at its hearth
and warm your hands in light.

The past is emotion spent
and motion arrested;
future is only prescience.

Home is this rising wind
cupping a sail,
storm, distance:
Heart's portent
pitted against a purpose
in the mind.

CHRISTMAS

Loves and homes within my head
confuse the living with the dead;
urgent gifts I almost bought
and sent (before I stopped and thought)
come back to deck the tinseled tree
like tokens from eternity.

SOLOMON'S RING

If I were not of human stuff
what worlds would open up!
To my quilled wing the hemisphere
were roving place enough;

or, naked but within my fur,
the lake my giant cup;

or, hurrying underground toward coal
where home waits snug in that deep hole,
thousands I interrupt;

or, moving on a fragile fin
behold a shell-starred sky
though stupefied the staring sight
within my shallow eye.

If I could change my high degree
of consciousness, of form,
for life that lives in water and earth,
in sky and tree --
I might come earlier to harm
of predators, of man, of storm,
or fail what prescience taught:

Enchant me yet to Solomon's Ring
where creature pulse and withering
go unimpaled by thought.

PILGRIM

Now this aftermath
upward. The clearing path
at twilight is patched with old snow
that fell I know not when
so curtained then
the world I left, toward which again I go.

Only the dwindling scars of lethal drifts
dappling my pungent earth with scattered white
spell in thin fossil shapes lost worlds of time.

Now up ahead remembered sky, my night
flung bold again, erupts from freed horizons,
quickens these limbs, this mind; I move in wonder
as though unlocked but now from Adam's rib.

TIME IS A TUNNEL

SCHOOL

Now let us praise the teacher
whose hand and tongue and pen
pardon the twisting creature
sudden beyond whose ken
the lesson veers from fractions
and far outside our room
forecasts the heart's transactions,
telescopes the tomb.

GUEST

I woke and saw a window
not my own
where starry wind
bore down the trees
and thrust
against my pillow
Saturn's silver ring.
I heard the sea
swelling, impending.
Rising, a tide
bore up the beach,
its dark waves breaking in,
fanning long arcs of shallow
on higher sand
like the slow fingers
of a shining hand
reaching for earth,
earth's creatures;
nearing me.

CONCOURSE

Asphalt or jungle path, no tributary's
too tortuous or mapped but it unites
with this impartial route
(imprinted by hoof, foot, belly, claw)
reeling its distance from geometry
straight to the journey's end, past Ultima Thule.

Our detours, corrected, equal destiny:
all roads feed this nameless span,
trajected highway.

In local trips we dream
angels of altitude above our foiliage, listen
for voices to sing us from the climate's wrack,
watch for a roadside cryptogram as guide,
challenge a wild terrain of mind and mountain;

but see how all perilous trails, all popular routes,
all interjecting ways between the oceans
straighten as one, succumb in infinity,
parallel forever the magnet concourse:

Time's luminous channel,
Time's Euclidian line.

ECHO AT THE GORGE

How ghostly back my question comes
I call into this void --
so ominous each syllable
my voice returns destroyed,
as though the chasm were a world
where centuries of men
their door of Limbo push ajar
and cry to earth again.

FOREBODING

Shifting and locking in the night
outside these station walls
what mighty wheels disturb my earth
with thundering rituals!

Waiting, I sleep, but still pervades
my mind a distant train
whose heavy engine in my dreams
bears down upon my brain
and head-on, like an eye of night,
its round and nearing stare
in huge dilation nears, till I
wake screaming in its glare.

Flame its fuel on trackless routes
and deeper night its goal
where hastening without Schedule
it rushes down my soul.

SEASCAPE

Same wavewash, same withering
beauty and blackness, wave on wave
where the struck beach lies lambent
bright dune, dark cave

in the same light, moonclouded,
whorling, rejoining overhead:
restive the room of earth, but O how quiet
love lies dead.

THE BURDEN

Cast your woe on the sun;
only in terrible fire, in holocaust
can such extremities of sense be lost
as feed this flaming pyre
streaming through heaven
where daily bring
ages of man his grief in offering.

Cast it you must, again, again,
though lessen never the granaries of pain
wherefrom your heart forever
takes its food.
There is no other nourishment
for whom would bear
longer the heavy pulse
of earth and air
and heaving sea
but this enormity.

Die, but put out the star
you knew was North;
sleep and moulder
in veinless earth
and know him worse
who moaning, kneels at night,
the Dipper bright
over his shoulder.

TIME'S TOUCH

Cling to this knowledge, vow in this hour
never to lose it, never grow blind again
having risen from sightlessness by will
and Time's touch, hold power
against the awful paucity of grief.

Heavy relief
gives back the world again, the season: gives
old clues to wind and water, the tight green leaf
uncurling, the meadow, the night's mood
starred and stirring.
What hooded host
curtained and prepared that interlude,
whispered, became a confidant, almost?

Now curved like the hills a lightening bridge of dawn
spans even the heart, proposes life again.

ACRE

Here below the quiet sod
white skulls have probed what they conceived,
white bones have found what flesh believed:
oblivion or God.

Stilled are all those intricate
philosophies and fragile schemes
called up by man against his dreams
of this, the ultimate.

Below the peaceful grass there lies
a world that kissed and spoke and wept
in time allotted, time that kept
terror in knowing eyes.

These who sleep below the sky
grow rich in what the living seek
albeit they cannot move nor speak
to bid us also die.

Deep-hid from snow and safe from sun
white bones do not protest the taut
dark thread that ravels back to naught
what birth had so begun.

OLD SORROW

Swift as an eagle lost in sky
(the claw, the beak, the silent wing)
a shadow, though I moved, stayed by
of that observed pursuant thing
that paced my progress. I bowed low
and knelt to wait and let it go
beyond me to its homing place.
It would not pass, but stopped in space.
It halted in infinity.
Its shadow lay across my face.

ATLANTIS

Lost Atlantis is my continent.
Deep on the ocean floor
her mountain peaks
jut in a sky of water,
persist, erode
in terrible pressures, ageless;
while down her plains
monsters with feathery fins,
dark, undulant,
flash from the shadows, live and die
unknown.
Wild carnage and beauty
lurk becalmed, attack,
silent and lost forever
where eagles nested;
and all her spreading sky
is filled with flood
and all her sun
millenniums arrested.

O but how bathed in early light she lay
when history had her
and nature loved her best,
and man on her green mountains
fed his heart –
by night on boundless love
and starry rest;
on innocent sunlight with his flocks
by day.

MIRAGE

I saw the city in a dream; I walked toward it
with other pilgrims. Unknown to one another
we trudged in the twilight, here and there
a thin line of movement, but mostly silent,
up a wooded hill, across a valley;
hastened in the bright morning; on, on, at noon.

We seldom spoke of it, or spoke at all; but saw
ahead in the sky (we thought) a golden radiance
tinting the white clouds, the blue midnight.

The dream was sure. Twice I beheld
sharply the living city from a summit:
Distant, O distant, but perfect, jewel-like,
struck by the sun. Again at dusk
in hazed beauty it urged the flowers
we carried concealed as secrets. Living, hastening.

There we saw home, our peace,
sun-tempered, flashing on prism windows.
Towers rose singly, loved by the sky.
Every street, cobbled and durable,
winding, led inevitably to a destination:
long-lost, unqualified, "Yes!"

GOD THE ARTIST

He is drugged with creation:
Time goes clockless by
His skillful hand,
uncompromising eye.

The Artist painting apples
none may eat,
His hungry children
listless at His feet . . .

WOMEN BY CANDLELIGHT

Lagging daylight through these rich portieres
urges up candlelight on samovars,
invests the tea with sacramental strength.
Evening, like omen, intensifies each face.

In muted acoustics, unheard the moment turns
surprised from time to its stopping point at dusk,
enchanted, enclosed, its corners filled with shadow.
Silver, embossed with splendid heraldries,
flickers in changing light, invites surmise.

Costumed women, stylized, revised, reviewed,
emerge like portraits in this darker mood,
buckles and plumes from history, the casual glove
momentous in artless fingers, the eyes
absorbed as though in rapture.
                                        This interlude
glows in a painted unity of color
and slow coherence of its dissonant sounds
electric and elemental.
                                        Gathered in
from hours of day and night, hid in this circle
as her in blue, with the brooch, the black feather,
I breathe less labored in a common weather
and feel brief ease in the rhythmless blur of words
wary of meaning, no, not even farewell.

As at some sylvan vesper where nestless birds
flown from their bright-plumed mates, their mates from them,
gather to drink at the pool's edge, hover
suddenly brilliant where strikes their dove-gray wings
such burning color as sunset seldom brings
we stand, delay, prolong the indecision,
ignore the issue, disturb the pool's dark mirror.

WINTER SUNSET

Above the peaked roofs and the spire – nearer
than my town and all my trees
(black spindles against, etched deep upon it)
always the sky impends:
cradle, crystal ball, fine ashes --
all is reflection, the infinite a stage
toward which we gaze and see ourselves transcended.
Now grief is a heavy golden cloud, moving,
heavy and golden to antipodes
the heart knows not, but follows; remembers
cumulous shapes in summer, enormous
white Alps, all glare,
towering, immobile . . .

EPILOGUE

COCKTAILS AGAIN...

COCKTAILS AGAIN

Once more we sit here in this Tavern's court
that used to be a speakeasy in the days
when Prohibition made of pubs a sport
outside the law. That far-back era plays
a phantom role in this, our get-together
in a year that telescopes the fervent past.
We're a different pair, in a different kind of weather,
at a rendezvous we've managed to keep at last.

This ailanthus tree -- it was just a struggling sapling,
and surrounding walls had no lichen on weathered stone.
But look how the twilight's luminous roseate dappling
filters about us, again makes the place our own.
Iris still grows; and of this table, mark
how rain has warped it, leaving its rough wood sere
with splinters on its once so smooth and dark
surface. One little leaf's imprisoned here,
preserved, perhaps, forever.
                                        Ah, my friend,
your eyes are sad. I know. It was last year,
last eon, maybe. What's it in the end
whether we sat here in our age or youth?
Memory? Yes, all retrospect is tinged

with some inexorable moment's flaming truth;
but the great epic sweep of life – is it not hinged
on these same moments? Shall we protest their dying
which opened up the Gate, albeit with pain?
(I can hear the echo of my old blood's crying.)
We are older now. We are having drinks again.

I read your thoughts. The girl you knew is dead
suddenly. You have met me. We are estranged
by the hovering phantoms of lovers. My head
tosses with no careless abandon. I am changed.

And you, my friend? I held your picture too,
straight and sure, clear-eyed. My heart mourns
in this moment, the other days we knew
of belief in Happiness and Unicorns.

I ask nothing now but sweet fables
sometimes to amuse my troubled brain;
sea waves, sunlight, ivy-covered gables,
the apocalyptic message of the rain.
My friend, I have killed windmills, I have shattered
the irrelevant ghosts which once loomed straight and tall
casting their shadows; I have long since battered
to dust a hoax, a high impregnable wall.

Disenchanted? No, I am merely calm
like the veteran of won or failured wars
who holds an insect in his calloused palm
and watches it traverse his sundry scars,
as small or great as was the enemy.

What have I then? Joy, but no joys, my friend;
and Sorrow but no sorrows. Ripeness brings
a clear untainted vision of Life's end;
I demand nothing for myself outside
those miracles I took for granted, turned
aside from fretfully: crisp leaves that died
and spread a brittle carpet; suns that burned
at dusk time; the cool creek and massive stone
where I once walked, unseeing. Those remain
ageless and wise with comfort.

I am alone,
my friend, though we have drinks again.

About The Author

Gladys Merrifield, born in Colton, California, a small town of the San Bernardino Valley, attended the University of California at Berkeley, where she was on the staff of the *Literary Review* and a frequent contributor of poems to that journal. In her junior year she won the Emily Chamberlain Cook Prize for Undergraduate Poetry offered by Professor Albert Stanborrough Cook of Yale in memory of his daughter. Judges were poets Robinson Jeffers and Witter Bynner, with Professor Benjamin P. Kurtz of the U.C. English Department. The prize poem "Sonnets Under a Roof," is included in this volume and was first published in booklet form by the University of California Press.

After college graduation she entered Columbia University in New York City, studying writing in the Graduate School. At the end of the year she joined the editorial staff of Dell Publishing Company, and met her future husband, the late Richard F. Merrifield, a magazine editor and writer. They moved to San Francisco, where their daughter was born.

A year later Gladys Merrifield won the James D. Phelan Fellowship in Literature, a $1,000 bequest stipulated in the will of the late Senator from California, for a work-in-progress. She was a regular contributor to poetry magazines and a member of a group of poets who gave readings of their works at the San Francisco Public Library. Among her other literary honors, she won the Robert Browning Award, offered by the Browning Society of California, for the title poem of this volume.

After residing in Keene, New Hampshire, she worked for 21 years in New York City as an editor and staff writer for *Family Circle*, the world's largest-selling women's magazine. In 1982, selections from the poems in this volume were read at Producer Joseph Papp's New York Shakespeare Festival in the Public Theatre as part of a monthly series called Poets at the Public. In the same year her work appeared in an anthology, *The View From the Top of the Mountain,* published by Barnwood Press. A long narrative poem, "The Roundabout Cafe -- Manhattan" won a Mason Sonnet Award from The World Order of Narrative Poets.

Gladys Merrifield is a longtime member of the Poetry Society of America, appearing in its *Diamond Anthology* in 1971. She is also a member of the Academy of American Poets. Her work has appeared in various magazines including *Wings, The Lyric West, Palms, Westward, The Fortnightly, Poet Lore, Reflections, Yankee, The Village Voice* . . .She believes with Kafka that "A book should serve as an axe for the frozen sea within us". Her favorite living writer is Samuel Beckett.

PUBLICATIONS
of
DRAGON'S TEETH PRESS

Living Poets' Series (Selected Titles):

Gustav Davidson, *All Things Are Holy*
Madeline Gleason, *Selected Poems*
Bernard Grebanier, *The Angel In The Rock*
Dorsha Hayes, *New Poems from the Bell-Branch*

Thomas Heffernan, *The Liam Poems*
Raymond Henri, *Dispatches From The Fields*
Cornel Lengyel, *Late News from Adam's Acres*
Sarah Lockwood, *New Lyrics*

Madeline Mason, *Sonnets In A New Form*
Jess Perlman, *Poems Past Eighty*
P.B. Newman, *Paula*
Robert L. Smith, *Refractions*

Thomas Thornburg, *Saturday Town*
Vasanti, *Mandala* 2^5
Wallace Winchell, *The House of Bethlehem*
William White, *Summer of Pure Ice*

DRAMA:

The Devil Comes to Wittenberg by George Hitchcock. Prize Play, New Poetic Drama, No. 1. $3.50.
The Case of Benedict Arnold by Cornel Lengyel. New Poetic Drama, No. 2. $3.50.

MUSIC (For Voice and Piano):

Fifty Songs by Ernst Bacon, with introduction by Paul Horgan. $10.
Hesperides by John Edmunds. Great lyrics set to music. $10.
Selected Songs by Jeanne Singer. Settings of modern American poets. $10.

PHILOSOPHY:

The Creative Self by Cornel Lengyel. Aspects of the artist's quest for self-knowledge and the springs of creativity. $5.
"One of the best books on creativity ever written."

–Corinne Geeting, WEST/ART

Order from:
DRAGON'S TEETH PRESS
EL DORADO NATIONAL FOREST
GEORGETOWN, CALIFORNIA 95634